C000000753

First published 1996
Revised edition © Wooden Books Ltd 2005

Published by Wooden Books Ltd.
8A Market Place, Glastonbury, Somerset

British Library Cataloguing in Publication Data
Martineau, John, 1967-
Mazes and Labyrinths in Great Britain

A CIP catalogue record for this amazing
object is available from the British Library

ISBN 1 904263 33 X

All rights reserved. For permission to
reproduce any part of this book in any form
whatsoever please contact the publishers.

Printed and bound in China
by R R Donnelley Asia Printing Solutions Ltd
100% FSC Certified sustainable papers.

MAZES AND LABYRINTHS

IN GREAT BRITAIN

by

John Martineau

To my Mother, Tess

*In this book most designs are shown with their entrance at the
bottom of the page regardless of their orientation in the field.*

*Other excellent books on Mazes and Labyrinths are by
W.H. Matthews, Nigel Pennick, Sig Lonegren and Jeff Saward.*

*Two modern mazes: Above, the Green Man Hedge Maze, 150' square,
Penpont, Brecon designed and planted by David Goff Eveleigh in 2000.
The frontispiece shows the Archbishop's Maze at Greys Court, Oxon, made for
the National Trust by Randall Coate and Adrian Fisher in 1984.*

CONTENTS

MAZES

Beware!
You *can* get lost

TROY TOWN
for catching smägubbar

The first section of this book deals with 'Mazes', designs in which you can get lost, where choices are offered to the walker and some paths may not lead to the goal; mazes are, by and large, a modern trend. 'Labyrinths', by contrast, the subject of the second and larger part of this book, are older, safer designs, which offer no choices, reliably delivering the faithful walker to the Centre every time as long as he or she stays on the path.

Troy Town, on the Scilly Isles, is the only ancient stone and boulder labyrinth in the British Isles (the diagram opposite is schematic and does not show the actual boulders). The construction is about 16 feet across and overlooks the sea.

In Norway, where more lore still exists concerning the use of these seaside designs, and where numerous examples still litter the cliffs and beaches, fishermen and sailors would walk labyrinths to ensure favourable winds and catches, and also to entrap *smägubbar*, gremlins or 'little people'.

Few ancient mazes and labyrinths retain the same design over the centuries. Reputedly built by the lighthouse-keeper, Amor Clarke, in 1729, Troy Town was altered in 1986 and again in 1989. The version shown does offer a small choice near the centre, but happily you still cannot actually fail to reach home.

MANUSCRIPT MAZE
five and eight

This maze design appears in a 17th century manuscript in the British Museum and is an excellent example of the increasing inventiveness and variation around the classical form which characterised the seventeenth and eighteenth centuries. As time went on, more and more choices were offered on the path, garden designers delighting in creations in which walkers, lovers and fools could get lost for hours.

Upon entering this maze, the aspirant chooses one of two paths, creating a sense of excitement, fear and trepidation. He or she knows not whether a dead-end lies ahead, or success. As the road travelled gets longer, the price of failure also grows. In fact, delightfully in this design, both routes lead to the centre, one slightly quicker than the other, useful for races!

A textbook example of good design, the circle here is elegantly and symmetrically divided into eight, and the graphic displays a wonderful balance between line and curve, light and dark. There are five circuits around the 'eye'.

Mazes with two solutions are quite rare. The only surviving ancient turf labyrinth in Germany has two entrances, a lime tree at its centre and is associated with lovers, dancers, sprinters and shoemakers, all common themes often found around these mysterious and engaging forms.

HAMPTON COURT
seven turns and an island

The Hampton Court maze is a true maze—you can get quite lost! The present hedges were planted in 1690 and the maze may be even older than that. At least twelve copies following the Hampton Court route have been built in the British Isles and over half a million people now walk the original each year.

The design was ahead of its time—it includes an 'island', a length of hedge in no way connected to the outer perimeter, making it harder to solve (*see pages 10-12*).

Go in, turn right, left twice, and then right four times to reach the centre. That makes seven turns. Or is that left and right upside down and back to front?

Shown below is a near copy which can be found under the west tower of St. Helena and St. Mary's church, Bourn, in Cambridgeshire. It dates from 1875. In 1912 the font was moved on top of the maze, rendering its confusions unwalkable.

ADAM ISLIP'S DESIGN
eight, square and circle

A Renaissance publication, *The Orchard and the Garden*, written by Adam Islip in 1602 contains the maze shown opposite. A bold and arresting design with three square circuits, four circular, and one between which is six of one and half a dozen of the other, it also boasts four secret triangular islands to hide, cuddle or snuggle in, or possibly get lost around. The total number of 'circuits' here is actually the octave, eight.

The theme of this pattern may later have been used by William Waldorf Astor who in 1905 planted a hedge maze very similar to this design at Hever Castle in Kent. The maze is still there today and marks the place where Henry VIII once courted poor Anne Boleyn. A stone labyrinth, also based on this design, can be found at Pahaluoto in Finland.

The design is one way of 'squaring a circle', where a circle (representing Heaven) and a square (representing Earth) are brought together in some intelligent manner. Here, various aspects of the circular heavens are explored, followed by a few corners of the earth, before a single choice is offered. One path leads to a dead end, the other to the central Oasis.

It should of course be remembered that, like so many things in life, no pictures, words or theories can ever really replace the experience of actually walking the path.

HATFIELD HOUSE
hand on wall

The yew maze at Hatfield House was planted in 1840. Situated to the east of the house, it is said to stand on the site of an earlier design. There are two entrances, one on the north side and one to the south, leading respectively to the west and the east sides of the central enclosure. If you reach the centre you must then decide whether to retrace your steps or cross the enclosure, beginning a new maze to find your way out. In this case you are not retracing your steps, and your memory, like Ariadne's thread, will be of no use. In a way this makes this maze a little like a labyrinth, as the outward journey will require the same amount of effort as the inward.

There is a secret way of solving mazes which is well worth knowing, an ancient trick known as the 'hand on wall' method. The technique requires that you simply follow the wall with your left (or right) hand, groping your way round corners, dead ends, and turning wherever your hand leads you, never taking your hand from the wall. You will eventually find yourself in the centre (or at least glued to its wall), and the exit.

The 'hand on wall' solution means that although superficially there seem to be dead ends here, on another level there are none. Mazes such as this can in fact be seen as labyrinths once you have the key.

CHEVENING
lost islands

By the nineteenth century the process of separation between the physical sciences and the metaphysical sciences was nearly complete in the west. Thus, instead of a path being simply something to follow in order to experience certain things in a certain order and so reach the centre, the route became confusing, and full of traps and pitfalls.

Despite this, as we have just seen, many early mazes could still be reduced to labyrinths and solved by the ingenious 'hand on wall' method. The example shown opposite, however, cannot be solved in such a way.

One of three innovative mazes designed by the Earl of Stanhope in the 1820's, it survives today at Chevening in Kent. A renowned mathematician, Stanhope realised that if elements of the design were isolated as 'islands', and not secured to the outer perimeter, then popular maze-solving tricks like the 'hand on wall' would not give the solution (try it!). Stanhope also spotted that the Hampton Court maze, dating back to 1690 (*see page 6*), was actually the first example of this principle.

This fiendish new development made the centre even harder to discover and unfortunately increased the number of people who could not find it.

CHATSWORTH HOUSE
five by six

The maze at Chatsworth House was planted in 1962 to an earlier design and stands on the site of the earlier Great Stove glasshouse. Like all good mazes and labyrinths it is at once a magical, subtle and beautiful place, somehow set apart for lovers of the mysteries. This particular design possesses four framed entrances and a small, sweet, central enclosure.

Unusually, the route can be wrongly taken even almost before starting. Of the four possible entrances into the circular maze from the rectangular surround, only one will prove fruitful. This is a feature unique to Chatsworth and wisely reminds the walker of the fact that the right road may need to be chosen from the very start if the preferred destination is to be gained.

The design seems to square the circle but is actually rectangular in plan, measuring an overall 35 by 41 yards. Of the five circular paths in the design, only four of them are complete, the fifth being interrupted by the linear perimeter. This may or may not allude to the *now you see it, now you don't* quality of the secret western fifth element of ether which was often set apart from the other four elements of fire, earth, air and water, themselves generally either arranged in a cross with the ether placed centrally, or outwards in concentric circles (the medieval 'sublunary spheres') with the ether outside, as here.

LEEDS CASTLE
the fine art of getting lost

In recent years a modern craze of maze and labyrinth building has taken over the country. A couple of examples are shown at the front of the book but this book is too small to show many more. The maze opposite was opened at Leeds Castle, Kent, in 1988. Laid out in yew, this crown design contains a multitude of islands and is quite a challenge. The successful explorer leaves through an underground grotto, caves and a secret passage.

The design has a few echoes of traditional design, and many departures too. There are numerous solutions here, none of them particularly meaningful, but all good *fun* (the modern *credo*). The division of the circuits into five circles and two squares may vaguely refer to the division of the week into five and two, itself based on the ancient heavenly scheme of Sun, Moon and five visible planets (fun for magicians).

One of the interesting things about modern mazes is the allegorical message that it is possible to get lost and fail on this fun journey to the centre, that the designer of the path may be out to trick you and keep you going round in circles. One must also consider how to get out again. These are good lessons.

The second part of this little book covers the older magical labyrinths of antiquity where a simple enchantment spell is cast and the mind may relax while the journey unfolds.

LABYRINTHS

Just follow
the path!

STRAIGHT LINES & CIRCLES
the hidden labyrinth

The common classical labyrinth has seven coils and is shown in one form opposite lower right and in it's traditional form on page 31. The top left image shows the standard spiral meander, another extremely ancient design. Both are found all over the world in many cultures and traditions, both speak of the relation between line and curve and they are closely related.

To get from one to the other, start with two units of a spiral meander (*1. top left*), imagining it to be made of stretchy stuff. Holding the right side rigid, pull the left side out and round one eighth of a circle (*2. top centre*), then one quarter (*3. top right*), then one half (*4. lower left*) and finally right around to create the complete design (*5. lower right*) The classical seven-coil labyrinth is thus already lurking in the spiral meander.

The importance of seven in the ancient world cannot be overstated. There are seven visible heavenly bodies which move across the stars, the Sun, Moon, Mercury, Venus, Mars, Jupiter and Saturn. These daily and nightly rise at various positions in the east and curve overhead to the south to later set in the west. Each used to be imagined as having its own shell, or sphere, around the Earth. To the medieval mind, walking a seven-coil labyrinth hinted at a journey to Earth (here, the centre) via these seven celestial spheres.

1.   2.   3.

4.   5.

THE WALLS OF TROY
a vanished turf labyrinth

Rockcliffe Marsh in Cumbria used to have a number of turf labyrinths. The beautiful design shown opposite was copied and drawn in 1883 when it was still visible, by R. Ferguson.

This pattern measured 24 by 26 feet with raised paths and cut gaps each about 8 or 9 inches wide. There are five coils wrapped round each side and eight coils vertically from the centre. Five and eight are often found to operate together in time and space, Venus's motions and timing around Earth being a good example. Here a three-coil heart-shaped spiral (turn the book upside down) must be walked before oscillating three times backwards and forwards over the centre.

This type of labyrinth, combining spiral and oscillating themes, is more commonly found in Scandinavian countries where they were associated with protection from depressing and clingy spirits of the dead. These poor lost souls reputedly could only travel in dead straight lines (down spirit paths, or ley lines) and so would get caught in the coils of these wonderful forms when the possessed human walked them. It is probably for this rather spooky reason that the folk name for a labyrinth in many countries is a 'spirit trap'. Spirits are also supposed to be incapable of crossing salt water, hence the special sanctity of islands and the centre of a labyrinth is still called its 'island'.

TARRY TOWN
sone Templar turns

Two miles outside Oxford lies the village of Temple Cowley and here was once found the most simple labyrinth in the country. The Order of the Knights Templar were once the landowners, and members of this erudite and secretive body used to walk the path as part of their initiations. The labyrinth was sadly destroyed in 1852.

This is the only example of a four-circuit labyrinth known to have existed anywhere in the British Isles; it measured sixteen and a half feet across.

As in all good labyrinths the walker initially heads straight for the centre but is diverted on a much longer journey in the process. A useful rhyme elaborating on this theme was reputedly recited by those walking this design:

> *So my boy, you wish to marry,*
> *Twere better far for you to tarry.*
> *Each one's load's enough to carry,*
> *And it's doubled when you marry.*

CAWDOR CASTLE

a modern double-meander

Far from being a dead art, traditional labyrinths have been springing up all over the country in recent years. The quartered nine-circuit design shown opposite is a good example. Originally a Roman mosaic design from Conimbriga in Portugal, it can now be found as a hedge labyrinth at Cawdor Castle, in Nairnshire, Scotland, where it was planted in 1981.

The form is known as a double-meander, which means that walker is required to zig-zag twice within each quarter before moving on to the next. There are no circumnavigatory paths and, enticingly, the walker is repeatedly presented with his or her proximity to the centre before finally getting there.

The Romans were keen labyrinth builders, and their mosaics often showed the hero Theseus at the centre, killing the terrible Minotaur. Daedalus, who designed the Minoan labyrinth, also used the pattern in a great dance floor he built for Aridane.

Try folding up the design like a fan from the bottom (*see page 21*), and you will get the double-meander border below.

HARPHAM

a triple meander

Five Roman labyrinths have been found in the British Isles to date and the one shown opposite is from Harpham in Yorkshire. Measuring eleven feet across it is dated to 304 AD and can now be seen at the City Hall of Kingston-upon-Hull in Humberside.

The design is known as a triple-meander, the quadrants each containing three repeats, the four being completed in an anticlockwise order. A similar Roman labyrinth found at Caerleon in Gwent can be seen in the Caerleon Museum. It too is a triple-meander but, unusually, the journey is clockwise.

The word *labyrinth* is obscure. It may or may not be relevant that the *Labrys*, the double-headed axe carried on a bundle of rods by Roman youths and carved into one of the stones at Stonehenge, has a shape roughly similar to the classical brain labyrinth described on the next page.

Then again, early Etruscan pitchers showing the labyrinth shape bear the word *Truia*, which means 'arena' or 'dance floor'. Sadly, Ariadne's dance is lost to history, and seems to already have deteriorated into 'The Game of Troy' by the time of Virgil. We can only wonder what role might have been played by Ariadne's thread, as the dancers of this game hypnotically moved in and out of her coils.

THE CITY OF TROY

a place of seven turns

On the verge beside the B1363 from Dalby to Terrington in Yorkshire can be found the last remaining ancient turf seven-coil labyrinth in the British Isles. The present cutting dates from the turn of the century. Labyrinths often go by the name of 'Troy' possibly because the Welsh *Caerdroia,* meaning 'the walls (or city) of Troy' can also be taken as *Caer y troiau,* 'The City of Turns'. This classical labyrinth occurs across the ancient world, on Greek coins, and on walls from Mexico to Spain, India to Ireland. The oldest examples are from Minoan Crete, dating from around 2500 BC. More recent examples include one carved on a rock face by the sea at Tintagel and a turf one on the coastal path between Looe and Seaton, both in Cornwall.

If the seven visible planets are superimposed in their traditional order (*see page 36*) then the magical journey goes as follows:

Mars is the first circuit to be walked *"I Will have a go at the Path"*, then Jupiter *"Wow! Amazing! So much!"*, then Saturn *"Restrictions! Time to learn and follow the Rules"*, then the circuit of the Sun *"Shine! The Lesser Mysteries are complete"*, then the Moon *"Give it back, reflect it in Measured amounts"*, then Mercury *"Communicate it with Wit, according to the Time, Place and Person"*, and finally Venus *"Always with Love and Beauty"*.

... and then there's the journey out again ...

TROY TOWN
fifteen spheres at Somerton

This labyrinth, at Somerton in Oxfordshire, is the only fifteen-coil classical labyrinth in the British Isles. Roughly sixty feet across, it sits in the grounds of Troy Farm beside the ancient Portway track.

The route takes the walker straight to the central cross and then requires the completion of the seven outer coils before the crossing is reached again. The seven inner coils are then walked before the aspirant can reach the sanctuary.

The geometry of this shape, and indeed that of all similar labyrinths, is strangely close to that of the common type-B flattened stone circle, 5000-year old examples of which litter ancient Britain. There are also enigmatic connections between this shape and the annual changing rising and setting positions of the Sun, Moon and planets from any given location. Like the heavenly bodies, the turnings come half the time in the north (the sun in summer and full moon in winter), the other half the time in the south (the winter sun and summer full moon).

There are fifteen circuits here, possibly reflecting the complete fifteen sphere system of medieval cosmology. These were, starting at the centre, the four elemental spheres, then the seven planetary spheres, and finally the four highest heavenly spheres (*see page 54 if you're keen*).

THE MIZ MAZE
nine coils on St. Catherine's Hill

The only square labyrinth to have survived from antiquity is the nine-circuit Miz Maze on St. Catherine's Hill, overlooking Winchester. Just under ninety feet wide it has a cut pathway, as opposed to the pathway being the raised dragon's-back of turf itself, the cuts separating the coils.

St. Catherine's Hill was fortified in the Iron Age, remained sacred throughout Roman times and was still the associated Holy Hill of the town in the twelfth century. St. Catherine, like St. Michael and St. George is associated with dragon-slaying, and her shrines are often on low hills beside a sacred spring. A small chapel once stood near the Miz Maze.

Beside St. Catherine's Hill lies Twyford Down on which the Kings of Wessex were crowned and where the 'dongas', an 8000 year-old system of huge ancient traders trackways used to meet. Twyford Down was unforgiveably destroyed for a motorway but the road-protest movement which was born there and within the nine coils of the Mizmaze remains a significant thorn in the planet-trashing tyres of many 'developers' to this day.

The ancient caskets of three kings were found while the cutting was being bulldozed. The skeletons were between eight and nine feet tall. Winchester College, which broke its solemn word never to sell the Down for 'development', might yet need its spirit trap.

HERBAL LABYRINTH
Thomas Hyll's design

This quartered seven-circuit design appeared in a book by Thomas Hyll in 1563. Entitled *A Most Briefe and Pleasaunt Treatyse Teachynge How to Dress, Sowe and Set a Garden*, the book contains two of Hyll's designs. During the 15th and 16th centuries labyrinths became extremely fashionable. The renaissance had not yet progressed to its expedient and materialistic conclusion and a little metaphysical advice still remained—here Hyll advised the careful planting of herbs according to the scheme of the seven visible heavenly bodies in their traditional order. Another version (*below*) once existed at Theobalds in Hertfordshire.

The ancient planetary order is given by the relative speeds of the heavenly bodies' motions against the stars. Earth is placed at the centre, and then, moving out, the spheres are the Moon (the fastest), Mercury, Venus, the Sun, Mars, Jupiter then Saturn (the slowest). Sadly, nowadays the Sun, like Westminster or Brussels, is the remote centre and few understand the heavens.

WATTS MEMORIAL CHAPEL
four quarters, seven turns and the arts & crafts

This labyrinth can be found inside the Watts Memorial Chapel, Compton, in Surrey. It is a copy of the famous seven-circuit pavement labyrinth at San Vitale, Ravenna in Italy.

The Chapel was built in 1896 by Mary Watts to her husband and is heavily influenced by the ideas of William Lethaby whose *Architecture, Mysticism and Myth* (1891) had argued persuasively for the reunion of the fine crafts with metaphysical studies.

It was due to Lethaby, William Morris and other luminaries of the day that the Royal College of Art came into existence. Little or no traditional metaphysics is taught in such places today, spawning an entire generation of artists and designers who have never heard of the seven heavens, let alone the golden section. We only have too look at the shallow and soulless world they sell us to see that there may yet be a case for studying the ancient jouney of the soul – and Labyrinths are a 'fun' way to start.

After a familiar initial dash at the centre the path wanders from the innermost coil outwards and inwards through coils one, two and three before processing out through all the coils to the seventh. From here the path moves slowly back in to the fifth coil, then out again to the seventh. Finally the way moves inwards coil by coil until, from the third, Venus again, the centre is suddenly found.

BATHEASTON

seven by seven seven by sevens

In 1985 this fascinating and enigmatic labyrinth was laid in the parish church of Batheaston near Bath, a copy of a medieval labyrinth, 44' 6" wide, which used to exist at the abbey of St. Bertin, Saint-Omer, Pas-de-Calais in France. The Batheaston version measures 16' 6" across (*see too page 24*).

The underlying structure is a grid of forty-nine by forty-nine squares. Forty-nine is of course the square of seven and the magic square of seven is traditionally associated with Venus, it's rows, columns and two primary diagonals adding up to 175 (5 × 5 × 7). This means that the subgrid here is a Venus square of Venus squares. Below we see the medieval Venus square shown with its odd and even numbers oppositely shaded to reveal a pattern we shall see again on page 58.

This design hides many other number games and secrets.

22	47	16	41	10	35	4
5	23	48	17	42	11	29
30	6	24	49	18	36	12
13	31	7	25	43	19	37
38	14	32	1	26	44	20
21	39	8	33	2	27	45
46	15	40	9	34	3	28

HARLEY MANUSCRIPT
an unusual design

This charming labyrinth appears in a tiny book amongst the many Harley manuscripts in the British Museum in London. Both this and the design on page 5 are thought to be the work of Viennese designer Ignaz Haas in the late seventeenth century. As with his other one, there is again here an excellent balance between the strong linear cross motif and the curved circular and diagonal elements.

Like many Roman designs, this labyrinth requires the person travelling it to complete each quarter in turn. A quarter begins with a long dash at the centre followed by a right-angled bounce all the way back out again. Following this the traveller must zig-zag from the outside in, and then from the inside out again before another mad dash at the centre kicks off the next quarter. Three quarters are completed in this fashion.

The fourth quarter is different. Here there is no right-angled bounce back after the initial lunge, but instead the quadrant is zig-zagged out and then back in again, to the third circuit of Venus, i.e. to Love and Beauty again, from where the Centre is then won.

Thus three headlong runs at the central temenos are gently deflected whilst one carefully planned approach is rewarded.

PIMPERNE

the object of the journey

This unique and unusual labyrinth once existed at Pimperne in Dorset, near Blandford. It was ploughed up in 1730, but was luckily recorded by the highly energetic antiquarian John Aubrey to whom we also owe the earliest sketches of the 5000-year old standing stones at Avebury.

Cut into the turf, the extraordinary path was bounded by one foot hight ridges. Writing in 1686, Aubrey states that it was "... much used by the young people on Holydaies and by ye School-boies."

The essentially triangular design is unique in Great Britain, as is the seemingly random spagetti-like nature of the coiling which is reminiscent of early Indian and African labyrinths. The only clue to its function is the tiny heart-shaped island at the centre, a reminder of the true purpose of life to any walker. The 'corners' are completed in an anticlockwise direction, starting with the bottom-left.

Having reached the centre, and stepping off the path, a further challenge could have presented itself here – finding a way out without crossing the path, possibly a useful trick for avoiding gremlins left behind in the coils.

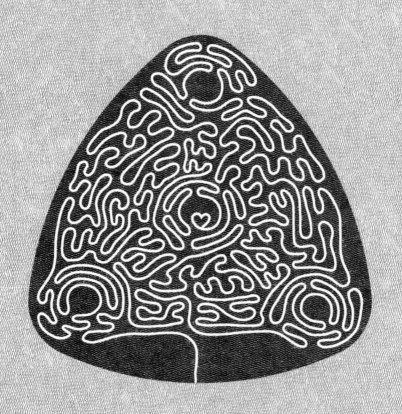

THE SHEPHERD'S RING
and a mischievous midsummer

Thirty-seven feet across, this labyrinth once existed on the village green of Boughton, near Northampton. It was one of many casualties of the First World War, destroyed by poor local soldiers (probably under instructions from their commanders) while practising trench-building in 1917.

The Ring seems to have been ancient and was traditionally run every year during the Midsummer Fair, which lasted for three days and three nights, and which had been held there at least from 1353 when it was granted by Edward III. Exhausted ring-runners, wrestlers and revellers would be refreshed and revived from the nearby St. John's Spring as the festivities peaked on St. John's Eve, the 23rd June.

The design is a delightful variant on the medieval 11-coil labyrinth (*see page 54-57*) with the outer eight circuits following the standard pattern while the inner three circuits (Venus, Mercury and the innermost Moon) simply forming an elegant spiral into the Earth. Thus the eleven is naturally divided into three and eight.

This can remind one, if one is so inclined, of the highly accurate rule of thumb that if the Earth is sized eleven, then the Moon is sized three.

SAFFRON WALDEN
the long jouney

The largest ancient labyrinth in the British Isles can still be seen on the village green in the delightful Essex town of Saffron Walden. It is surrounded by a ditch and mound and measures about 120 feet across. The pathway is a staggering one mile long and there used to be an ash tree on the large central mound. (the diagram opposite is schematic).

As at the St. Catherine's Hill Mizmaze, the path consists of the groove instead of the raised turf, and at Saffron Walden this is now a narrow red brick path,

The four strange corner protrusions were known as 'bastions' and point towards the nearby market towns of Newmarket, Chelmsford, Bishop's Stortford and Cambridge. The design is unique, having 17 circuits. Legend has it that an even larger labyrinth once existed further to the east.

As at many other labyrinths there used to be a custom that a maiden would stand at the centre while her beau would try and run the whole design without putting a foot wrong. Legends then vary: some say he was allowed to dance with her, while others suggest he had to carry her all the way out of the labyrinth if he wished to keep her.

This might have been no small task at Saffron Walden.

ROBIN HOOD'S RACE
another lost treasure

This ancient labyrinth used to sit on the summit of a hill near St. Anne's holy well, Sneinton, from which, it is recorded, flowed the purest and most healing water in all Nottinghamshire. The entrance seems to have been in the west.

The pathway was, like Saffron Walden, a trench between raised turf banks and was said to have been 535 yards long; the design has also been recorded as measuring one hundred feet across. The corner bastions contained crosses, crosslets or 'fitchies' cut into the turf.

Robin Hood's Race was ploughed up in 1797 as the new enclosures removed common rights to common land from common people, a process which is still in vogue all over the world, and shows no sign of slowing. The association between good clean water, free access and fun may have something to do with it.

The design is a slight variation on the medieval eleven-circuit pattern (*see pages 54-57*), probably a result of errors introduced in various recuttings. In this version is has a quick exit route, or, if you want to cheat, a fast entrance!

ELY CATHEDRAL
a dragon coiled up five by eight

In 1870 this labyrinth was laid in the stone pavement under the west tower of Ely Cathedral in Cambridgeshire. As in the case of the medieval labyrinth at Chartres Cathedral (*see page 56*) the length of the winding pathway is the same as the length of the cathedral.

The design is peculiar to Ely and was the work of Sir Gilbert Scott, another member of the Arts and Crafts movement (*see page 38*). A five-circuit dynamic square with protruding three-circuit octagons, it bears little obvious similarity to any known medieval labyrinth but again refers to a connection between five and eight (*see pages 4 & 22*).

The tradition of having labyrinths in the west end of cathedrals is prevalent in France where priests would dance their way to the centre (Jerusalem), three steps at a time, having first formed a chain. The dean went first, occasionally throwing a large ball to priests caught elsewhere in the labyrinth who would then throw it back to him. The ball seems to have symbolised the Sun, or possibly the Moon, both newly hidden behind huge stone buildings.

British monks also walked mazes and labyrinths, but more often as penances, or allegorical pilgrimages.

THE SHOEMAKERS' RACE
through the dragon's coils to the green man

This turf labyrinth was first cut by the Patriotic Company of Shoemakers at Kingsland near Shrewsbury in 1598 but was destroyed in 1796 to make space for a windmill. On reaching the centre the walker or runner is reported to have had to jump on to 'the Giant's Head', a great green face cut into the central turf, with one heel in each eye.

The design is an octagonal version of the medieval eleven-circuit labyrinth. Eleven was the total number of heavenly spheres in the medieval cosmos. Around the seven spheres of the planets (*see page 36*) four outer spheres were to be found - the sphere of the fixed stars (the stations), the sphere of the sky without stars (the zodiacal signs), the sphere of the Divine Pedestal and the sphere of the Divine Throne. These four outer spheres were sometimes balanced by four inner elemental spheres - Fire (or Ether), Air, Water and Earth, making fifteen in all (*see page 32*).

Eleven and seven, the two most common labyrinth numbers, also relate to each other as the circumference of a circle does to its diameter, thus again relating the line and the curve, masculine and feminine, heaven and earth,

A twelve-sided, 40 foot version of this design also once existed between the villages of Paul and Marfleet in Yorkshire.

THE 11-COIL LABYRINTH
the universal medieval maze

The earliest and most famous eleven-coil medieval labyrinth is found on the floor of Chartres Cathedral near Paris, the same size as the huge rose window above it, positioned the same distance from the wall as the window is from the floor, and with a path length equal to the length of the cathedral.

Luckily, there are a few turf versions of the pattern still left in Great Britain. One, measuring 55 feet across, is on the village green of Hilton, Cambridgeshire. Another, 50 feet wide, can be seen at Wing in Leicestershire. A famous version, Julian's Bower, overlooks the spot where the rivers Trent and Humber meet near Alkborough, Humberside. Perhaps the most beautiful of all is the Mizmaze at Braemore House, near Salisbury, where the labyrinth sits deep in a clearing in sleepy woodland.

There are 28 half-moon turns and four quarter-turns in the design; the folded version is shown below (*see pages 20-21*).

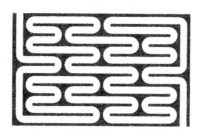